W9-BZS-893

DISCARD

Vanishing RAIN FORESTS

BY PAULA HOGAN

ENVIRONMENT ALERT!

J333.75
HOG

DISCARD

DISCARD

Gareth Stevens Children's Books
MILWAUKEE

For a free color catalog describing Gareth Stevens' list of high-quality children's books, call 1-800-341-3569 (USA) or 1-800-461-9120 (Canada).

Library of Congress Cataloging-in-Publication Data

Hogan, Paula Z.
    Vanishing rain forests / Paula Hogan.
      p. cm. — (Environment alert!)
    Includes bibliographical references and index.
    Summary: Discusses rainforest ecology and its worldwide destruction, using the Amazon Basin as a case study.
    ISBN 0-8368-0477-5
    1. Rain forest ecology—Juvenile literature. 2. Deforestation—Environmental aspects—Juvenile literature. 3. Rain forest conservation—Juvenile literature. [1. Rain forest ecology. 2. Ecology. 3. Deforestation. 4. Rain forest conservation.]
I. Title. II. Series.
QH541.5.R27H64   1991   91-3082

A Gareth Stevens Children's Books edition

Edited, designed, and produced by
Gareth Stevens Children's Books
1555 North RiverCenter Drive, Suite 201
Milwaukee, Wisconsin 53212, USA

Text, artwork, and format copyright © 1991 by Gareth Stevens, Inc. First published in the United States and Canada in 1991 by Gareth Stevens, Inc. All rights reserved. No part of this book may be reproduced in any form or by any means without permission in writing from Gareth Stevens, Inc.

Picture Credits
AP/WIDE WORLD PHOTOS, p. 16 (upper); Dave Augeri/Greenpeace, © 1990, pp. 12, 21 (upper), 25; © Nair Benedicto, D. Donne Bryant Stock, pp. 15, 24 (lower); © Cynthia Brito, D. Donne Bryant Stock, p. 17 (left); Al Buchanan, D. Donne Bryant Stock, © 1987, pp. 26-27; © Third Coast Stock Source, pp. 4, 5, 10-11, 18; © Michael Fogden/DRK PHOTO, p. 11 (lower); J. Heitchue/Greenpeace, © 1990, p. 24 (upper); © Nathan Kraucunas, pp. 2-3, 17 (right), 22, 25 (inset), 27; Mark Mille/DeWalt & Associates, pp. 6-7, 19; © James D. Nations, D. Donne Bryant Stock, p. 14; Pat Ortega, pp. 8-9 (insets); © Chico Paulo/Third Coast, cover; Campbell Plowden/Greenpeace, © 1990, pp. 8-9, 23; Reuters/Bettmann, p. 16 (lower); Meg Ruby/Greenpeace, © 1989, p. 13 (both); Tim Spransy/Dodge Design, pp. 28-29; Kennan Ward/DRK PHOTO, © 1989, p. 11 (upper); John Werner, © 1989, cover (inset) and pp. 20, 21 (lower).

Series editors: Kelli Peduzzi and Patricia Lantier-Sampon
Series designer: Laurie Shock
Book designer: Sabine Huschke
Picture researchers: Daniel Helminak and Diane Laska
Research editor: Jamie Daniel
Editorial assistant: Scott Enk

Printed in the United States of America

    4 5 6 7 8 9 97

At this time, Gareth Stevens, Inc., does not use 100 percent recycled paper, although the paper used in our books does contain about 30 percent recycled fiber. This decision was made after a careful study of current recycling procedures revealed their dubious environmental benefits. We will continue to explore recycling options.

Production Director

President

CONTENTS

Words that appear in the glossary are printed in **boldface** type the first time they appear in the text.

THE GREENBELT OF LIFE

Above: The anthurium plant grows in the rain forest of the West Indies.

Tropical **rain forests** are the most alive places on Earth. They are home to half of all living **species**. Rain forests receive 160 to 400 inches (400-1,000 cm) of rain each year. Temperatures stay near 80°F (27°C).

Rain forests are storehouses of riches, such as lumber, medicines, foods, and rubber. Rain forests play an important part in world weather patterns and are home to wildlife found nowhere else. Yet today, rain forests are rapidly being lost. Every year, 50 million acres (20 million ha) are burned, cut down, or bulldozed. That's more than a football field each second! At this rate, all rain forests will be gone by the year 2007. When the rain forests vanish, so do their plants and animals. Some people think that up to 17,000 different species have been completely wiped out.

Half of all the rain forests that ever existed have been destroyed, but people around the world are working to save the 800 million acres (320 million ha) that are left. Some countries, such as Brazil and Thailand, have set aside parts of their rain forests as protected areas. But much more needs to be done if rain forests are to survive.

Opposite: Even though the world's rain forests are home to half of all species, rain forests cover less than 7 percent of the Earth's surface.

A Storehouse of Riches

Rain forests provide many products that are used by people around the world. Coffee, bananas, rice, and cinnamon began as rain forest plants. Medicines that fight cancer, heart disease, and other illnesses are made from rain forest plants. Rubber is tapped from rain forest trees.

Many of these crops now grow on farms. Yet we still need their wild cousins to improve their quality. Rain forest coffee and sugarcane plants, for example, were bred with those raised on plantations. The result was crops that could fight off diseases. Who knows what other products rain forests could provide if they are saved?

NORTH AMERICA

CENTRAL AMERICA

SOUTH AMERICA

Far right: Tropical rain forests circle the globe. They are found in South America, Asia, Africa, Australia, and Central America. Even the United States and its territories have rain forests — in Hawaii, Puerto Rico, the U.S. Virgin Islands, and American Samoa.

Right: Rain forests give us many useful and beautiful products, including violets, orchids, **latex** (rubber), coffee, bananas, medicinal plants, coconuts, oils, and **rattan**. (The items shown in this illustration are not drawn to scale.)

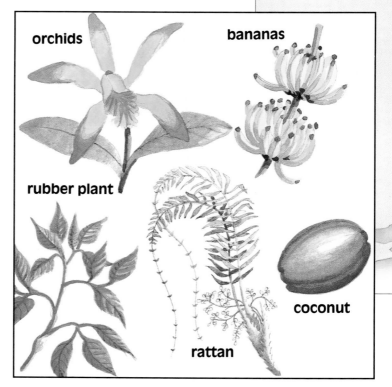

orchids

bananas

rubber plant

coconut

rattan

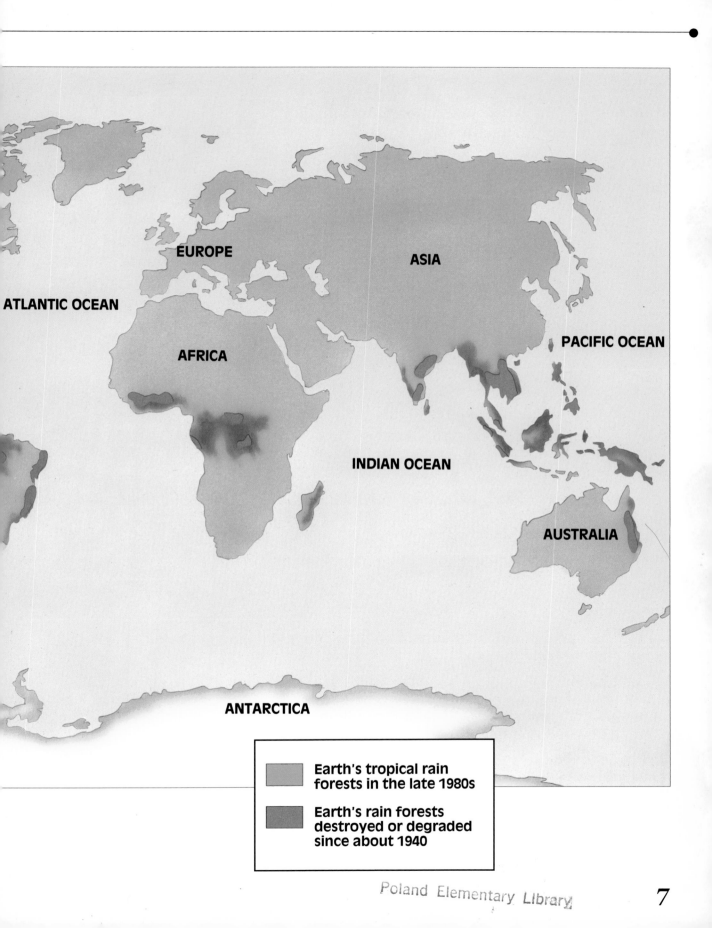

EUROPE

ASIA

ATLANTIC OCEAN

AFRICA

PACIFIC OCEAN

INDIAN OCEAN

AUSTRALIA

ANTARCTICA

Earth's tropical rain forests in the late 1980s

Earth's rain forests destroyed or degraded since about 1940

Poland Elementary Library

Layers of Life

Animals live at different heights in rain forest vegetation, and animals that live at one level seldom travel to another. The yellow-casqued hornbill (1), the colobus monkey (2), and the blue fairy flycatcher (3) make their home primarily in the forest canopy. The Jameson's mamba (4) and the chimpanzee (5) live in the understory. The okapi (6), the leopard (7), and the Congo peafowl (8) live on the forest floor.

Plant life in tropical rain forests grows in layers. At the very top, a few trees poke out of a thick tangle of vines, flowering plants, and treetops called the **canopy**. Most of the animals of the rain forest, including monkeys, birds, and tree frogs, live in the canopy.

Below the canopy is a mass of young trees and shrubs that make up the **understory**. Many plants in this layer never grow to adult size because the canopy blocks out most sunlight. Tiny **tamarins** and **marmosets** live in the understory.

The forest floor is almost bare because few plants can grow in the dim light. Yet trillions of cockroaches, ants, and termites swarm along the ground. These creatures play a key role in enriching the soil. They feed on dead plants and animals, making them decay faster. In this way, the **nutrients** from this dead material are returned to the soil to help new plants grow.

Large mammals also live on the forest floor. The biggest of these are the African and Asian elephants. African gorillas are too heavy to climb high into the canopy. Jungle cats, such as the South American jaguar and the leopard of Africa and Asia, also live on the ground.

A Huge Web of Wildlife

Abundant warmth and rainfall make it possible for an enormous number of plants and animals to thrive in a rain forest. In Borneo's rain forest, for example, 2,500 species of trees grow in an area half the size of Great Britain. Compare that with the 35 species of trees that grow in *all* of Great Britain, or the 865 kinds of trees on the entire North American continent.

Plants in a rain forest are at greater risk of **extinction**, however, than plants in other areas. Forests in colder climates have fewer species of plants, but a lot of each species. In tropical rain forests, there are many different species, but only a few of each kind. If even a small area of rain forest is cleared, many species could be wiped out.

One of the most interesting things about rain forests is not what we know about them, but what we *don't* know. Perhaps thousands of species of plants and animals have not yet been discovered. If rain forests continue to be destroyed, thousands of species will be lost before we ever learn about them.

Colorful bromeliads are found in the rain forests of Costa Rica.

Some 2,600 species of birds nest in rain forests. The keel-billed toucan lives in the rain forest of Guatemala.

This pair of spider monkeys lives in Panama's rain forest canopy. One drinks from a balsa flower.

Vanishing Tropical Rain Forests

Every year, over 78,000 square miles (202,000 sq km) of rain forest disappear. That's an area the size of Nebraska or almost three times bigger than the Province of New Brunswick. At this rate, all rain forests will be destroyed by the year 2007.

Logging is the main cause of rain forest destruction in Asia and Africa. In Ghana, the Ivory Coast, and Thailand, logging has destroyed over 80 percent of the rain forests. Rain forest woods are made into furniture, building materials, paper, packaging, and even disposable chopsticks.

Below: The rain forests in Borneo are vanishing because of too much logging. After the trees are gone, the land can be used for farming for only a short time.

Farming also causes **deforestation**. Hundreds of thousands of poor people in South America and Indonesia are trying to farm in the rain forest. But forest soil is not rich enough. After a few years, the soil loses its nutrients, and so farmers must leave their fields and clear new ones. Sadly, their old fields are too big, and there are too many of them, to allow the forest to grow back.

Ranching Devastation

Cattle ranching has destroyed more rain forest in Central and South America than any other human activity. Rain forest cleared for pasture seldom grows grass — or anything else — for over seven years.

Left: This Costa Rican farm was once covered with rain forest. After the forest was cleared, the soil eroded.

FACT FILE
Tragedy in the Amazon Basin

The rain forest of South America's Amazon River Basin seems to stretch endlessly. Yet it will soon disappear because of human greed and carelessness.

The Brazilian government has borrowed millions of dollars from the World Bank and other lenders to pay for development projects. Road building has opened up the rain forest to logging, mining, and farming. These activities quickly lead to **topsoil erosion**. Neither crops nor rain forest can grow without topsoil, so farms are soon abandoned. In this way, the fertile forest becomes a barren wasteland.

Over 1.5 million acres (600,000 ha) of rain forest in Ecuador are used for oil production. Another 7.5 million acres (3 million ha) are being explored for oil. Waste oil and mud poisoned by drilling are pumped back into streams. These **toxins** poison drinking water, killing people and wildlife. Some oil wastes are burned, polluting the air.

Most oil development is in national parks, wildlife reserves, and near native villages. **Environmentalists** demand that the oil companies leave the forest alone. Only if we slow the development of the Amazon will its native peoples and species survive.

Above: Development projects, such as this oil camp in Napo, Ecuador, clear huge parts of the fragile rain forest.

Opposite: The Amazon rain forest is home to over 10 percent of all living creatures. Tragically, it is being burned and cut at a frightening pace.

The Story of Chico Mendes

Chico Mendes was a poor rubber tapper living in the Brazilian rain forest. In 1969, the government began building roads, and thousands of people moved in to clear the forest and set up farms and cattle ranches.

The government wanted the rubber tappers to leave. Chico Mendes said no. He convinced his fellow workers of their right to stay. After all, they had been there first, and rubber tapping hadn't damaged the rain forest.

Chico Mendes and his friends formed human roadblocks to stop bulldozers from clearing the forest. Chico formed a workers' union and set up rain forest reserves for harvesting products that don't harm the forest.

The ranchers hated Chico Mendes because he kept them from enlarging their ranches. Mendes knew he was in danger, but he did not stop trying to save the rain forest. On December 22, 1988, Chico Mendes was shot and killed by a rancher's son.

Chico Mendes died a hero. His hopes for the rain forest live on in the work of conservation groups, native tribes, and ordinary people.

Chico Mendes was a brave rubber tapper who sacrificed his life to save the rain forest.

Chico's wife, Ilzamar Mendes, continues the work her husband started.

Above: A rubber tapper gathers sap from rubber trees. Rubber tapping is a good source of income because the trees can be tapped many times without harming the rain forest.

Right: Latex, or rubber sap, trickles out of a rubber tree. The rubber can be made into many goods, but tapping the tree does not harm it.

When Rain Forests Die

The rain forest's lush plant cover helps to create its moist, tropical climate. A tree draws water up through its roots to the leaves. Later, it breathes the water out of the leaves and into the air. This water falls back to Earth as rain. If too much plant cover is lost, less rain will fall. Without enough moisture, the rain forest can't live.

Below: Often, rain forests are burned to clear land for farms. These fires add 2.5 billion more tons of **carbon dioxide** to the **atmosphere** each year!

When too many trees die, the world's weather changes. Rain forests help keep the Earth cool by absorbing a great deal of carbon dioxide, a gas in the Earth's atmosphere. Carbon dioxide gets into the air from forest fires, engine exhausts, and factory smokestacks. It traps the Sun's heat, just like a greenhouse traps heat.

When forests are cleared, there are fewer trees to absorb carbon dioxide from the air. With more carbon dioxide in the air, the Earth's temperature may rise. This warming is called the greenhouse effect. It could lead to spreading deserts, **drought**, polar melting, coastal flooding, and other crises.

Below: To stay cool, the Earth needs its forests to filter harmful gases from the atmosphere. These gases come from the burning of fuel by industries, cars, and trucks. Without trees to filter the gases from the air, the gases form a layer around the Earth and trap heat from the Sun. This is called the **green-house effect** and may cause our planet to become too warm to grow crops.

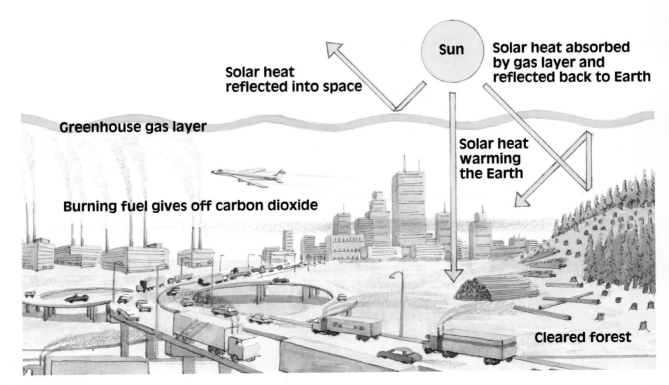

Solar heat reflected into space

Sun

Solar heat absorbed by gas layer and reflected back to Earth

Greenhouse gas layer

Solar heat warming the Earth

Burning fuel gives off carbon dioxide

Cleared forest

Endangered Native Cultures

Extinction Hurts Us All

Up to 17,000 plant and animal species have become extinct as rain forests have disappeared. Many more are endangered, such as this orangutan of Borneo. Yet, with so many species living in rain forests, why should we care if some vanish forever?

We must care because all species depend on each other to survive. For example, insects spread pollen from one plant to another, helping plants reproduce. These plants are eaten by some animals, which in turn are eaten by meat-eating animals. When one species vanishes, others suffer or disappear, too.

Right: The Penan tribespeople of Malaysia are trying to stop loggers from cutting down their forest home. In 1987, they blocked a logging road. The government put many Penan in jail and let the logging continue.

Opposite: A Penan tribesman.

The world's rain forests are home to over 1,000 groups of native peoples. Many follow traditions that are thousands of years old. They know which plants are good for food or medicine. They are also able to raise crops in the rain forest without harming it.

These native peoples have much to teach us about the rain forest. Yet their cultures have become endangered by farmers, loggers, miners, and ranchers, who have destroyed the natives' forest home. Many natives are forced into camps and must adapt to life in the modern world. Many others die of diseases brought in by the outsiders. These people deserve to live as they always have, just as we deserve to live our own life-style.

SAVING THE RAIN FORESTS
Using Rain Forests Wisely

Earth has about 5.3 billion people, and the number grows every day. Most of this growth is happening in tropical countries. Having all these new mouths to feed has led to clearing rain forests for farmland. In Indonesia and Brazil, governments have moved people from crowded areas to rain forests so that they have more room to grow food. These governments are also taking steps to provide better health care for the people who live there, along with proper education about population control.

Below: Native forest peoples practice intercropping. That is, they grow many crops together in one small field to improve yields and reduce insect pests. This field contains both coffee bushes and banana trees.

People could also learn to make a living from the rain forest without harming it. In the African nation of Cameroon, for example, government and **conservation** groups have set up a buffer zone around the Korup rain forest. There, local people and scientists experiment with less harmful farming and logging methods. They also look for new products to make from rain forest plants.

Above: Brazil has set up an 8,000-square-mile (20,700-sq-km) reserve. There, products such as nuts, oils, latex, and rattan are harvested without damaging the Amazon rain forest.

Foreign Loan Dangers

The World Bank loans money to developing nations. These loans fund projects that are supposed to help people. Sadly, many of these projects harm rain forests. The loans pay for dams that flood rain forests and drive out wildlife and native peoples. Highways built with foreign funds open the forests to loggers and farmers.

Most of the World Bank's loans go to wealthy ranchers, loggers, and mining companies. Also, companies from richer countries sell machinery for these projects and make money from the loans.

Some of these projects have been stopped. Environmental groups and local people stopped the building of 79 dams and a nuclear power plant in the Amazon Basin alone!

Above: People in Washington, D.C., protest against the World Bank. The bank makes loans to companies that use the money for projects that destroy rain forests.

Opposite: Logging companies cut hundreds of miles of roads through the rain forest of Borneo with the help of loans from foreign banks.

Left: Gold miners toil at the Serra Pelada gold mine in Brazil. Mining strips the land bare of rain forests.

"Debt-for-Nature" Trades

To pay back their huge loans, rain forest countries produce goods, such as beef and timber, to sell overseas. Producing such goods destroys the rain forest, however, and doesn't really help the people who live in those countries.

To prevent rain forest destruction, some conservation groups are paying off parts of these loans. In return, countries such as Bolivia and Costa Rica have promised to set aside parts of their rain forests as protected reserves. This arrangement is known as a debt-for-nature trade.

A Worldwide Effort

People around the world are worried about rain forest destruction. They are joining conservation groups that work to stop it. These groups pressure governments in tropical countries to preserve their rain forests. Friends of the Earth, for example, convinced the Malaysian government not to build a dam in the Tanan Negara rain forest.

Conservation groups also fund projects that benefit rain forests. The World Wide Fund for Nature buys up rain forest land. This organization fences it in, teaches local people how to harvest rain forest crops, and protects native rain forest dwellers.

Some companies are looking for ways to help. An ice-cream maker sells a flavor with Brazil nuts, a product harvested from rain forest trees. A cereal company is testing rain forest ingredients for its breakfast products. Some restaurants are refusing to buy beef raised on former rain forest land for their hamburgers.

Rain forests are like no other place on Earth. Their beauty and vast number of plants and animals can never be replaced. It is vital that people everywhere work to save the rain forests. For if we lose this wonderful environment, life will be poorer for all of us.

Above and opposite: Tourism can help save rain forests. Local people earn a living from the money that tourists spend when they visit, instead of farming or logging in the forest.

RESEARCH ACTIVITIES

1. **Create your own tropical rain forest.**
   Fill any clear glass container with a layer of sand or gravel. Top this with potting soil. Plant ferns, African violets, and other tropical plants. Water well and seal the top with clear plastic. Put in a partly sunny spot. The terrarium keeps itself watered, just like a rain forest does!

2. Make a list of endangered rain forest species.
Glue or draw pictures of each species next to its name. How many species of plants and animals are endangered?

3. Visit a botanical garden.
Make a list of the plants that grow in the rain forest. How many plants can you list? Draw a picture of your favorite rain forest plant.

4. Hold a contest to design a rain forest conservation poster.
How many ways to save the rain forest can you show?

Things You Can Do to Help

The following activities will help protect rain forests. Try to involve your friends, family, and classmates in your conservation efforts.

1. **Make a list of rain forest products.** Show which ones harm the rain forest and which ones don't. Post this list in your classroom or school. Ask your friends not to buy or use products that harm the rain forests.

2. **Conserve on products that you use.** Eat beef less often, use less paper, and recycle what you use. Don't buy clothing made from the skins and hides of rain forest animals.

3. **Build a bird sanctuary.** Many birds migrate from the north to the rain forests for the winter. Provide these little travelers with a rest stop by putting up bird feeders. For more information about how to do this, write to the National Wildlife Federation's Backyard Wildlife Habitat Program, 1400 16th Street NW, Washington, D.C. 20036.

Places to Write for More Information

The following organizations work to save the rain forests. When you write to them for more information, be specific about what you want to know.

Rainforest Action
  Network
301 Broadway, Suite A
San Francisco, California
  94133

Rainforest Alliance
270 Lafayette Street
New York, New York
  10012

Greenpeace (Canada)
2623 West 4th Avenue
Vancouver, British
  Columbia V6K 1P8

More Books to Read

Animals of the Tropical Forests, by Sylvia A. Johnson (Lerner Publications)
The Great Kapok Tree, by Lynne Cherry (Harcourt Brace Jovanovich)
Rain Forest, by Helen Coucher (Farrar, Straus & Giroux)
The Tropical Rainforest, by Jean Craighead George (Crowell)
Wonders of the Rain Forest, by Janet Craig (Troll Associates)

Glossary

atmosphere — the layer of gases surrounding the Earth

canopy — the topmost layer of plant life in the rain forest

carbon dioxide — a common gas in the Earth's atmosphere

conservation — saving the environment from spoilage or destruction

deforestation — the clearing of an area of trees

drought — the drying of the land due to a lack of rainfall

environmentalists — people who work to protect nature

extinction — the dying out of all members of a plant or animal species

greenhouse effect — the warming of the Earth caused by a buildup of gases in the atmosphere that trap the Sun's heat

latex — the milky sap of the rubber tree

marmosets — very small monkeys with thick, soft fur

nutrients — substances needed for life and growth

rain forests — forests near the equator that receive 160 to 400 inches (400-1,000 cm) of rain per year, with stable temperatures around 80°F (27°C)

rattan — the stems of climbing palms that are woven into furniture

species — a group of living things with the same physical characteristics

tamarins — small monkeys with silky fur and long tails

topsoil erosion — the loss of the upper layer of soil from wind and water

toxins — poisons

understory — the layer of plant life directly beneath the rain forest canopy

Index